American Moments

ABDO
Daughters

THE SPACE SHUTTLE COLUMBIA DISASTER

By Rachel A. Koestler-Grack

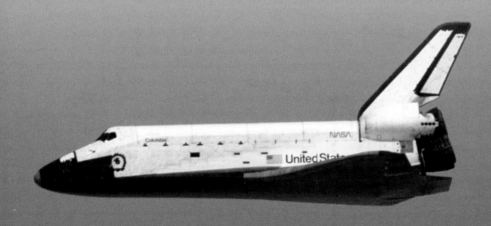

VISIT US AT
WWW.ABDOPUB.COM

Published by ABDO Publishing Company, 4940 Viking Drive, Suite 622, Edina, Minnesota 55435. Copyright ©2004 by Abdo Consulting Group, Inc. International copyrights reserved in all countries. No part of this book may be reproduced in any form without written permission from the publisher.

Printed in the United States.

Edited by: Alan Pierce
Contributing Editor: Melanie A. Howard
Interior Production and Design: Terry Dunham Incorporated
Cover Design: Mighty Media
Photos: Corbis, Kennedy Space Center

Library of Congress Cataloging-in-Publication Data

Koestler-Grack, Rachel A., 1973-
    The Space Shuttle Columbia disaster / Rachel A. Koestler-Grack.
        p. cm. -- (American moments)
    Includes index.
    ISBN 1-59197-659-6
    1. Columbia (Spacecraft)--Accidents--Juvenile literature. 2. Space vehicle accidents--Juvenile literature. [1. Columbia (Spacecraft)--Accidents. 2. Space shuttles--Accidents.] I. Title. II. Series.

TL867.K64 2004
363.12'465'0973--dc22
                                                                                                    2003069502

CONTENTS

SIXTEEN MINUTES FROM SAFETY

On February 1, 2003, the seven astronauts aboard the space shuttle *Columbia* finished the last systems checks. They radioed Mission Control in Houston, Texas, to say that the ship was in the correct position for reentry. They were preparing to return home.

Computers guided *Columbia* during most of the reentry. Flying a shuttle through reentry and landing usually goes smoothly. But it is challenging. Many astronauts have acknowledged the difficulty of returning a space shuttle to Earth.

Pilot William C. McCool and Mission Commander Rick Husband took over from the computers after the ship passed through what is called the plasma stage. Keeping control of the ship during this part of the return is tricky. McCool and Husband maneuvered the orbiter in S-turns to slow it down. At the same time, they monitored dozens of dials and indicators to make sure the ship stayed on course.

At 8:45 AM eastern standard time, *Columbia* began to enter Earth's atmosphere. Atmospheric friction created a pink glow around the shuttle as the protective tiles on the ship heated up. The glow changed from pink to red to scorching white as the ship continued its rapid descent. During reentry, the tiles heated to almost 3,000 degrees Fahrenheit (1,650°C). At this time, *Columbia*'s reentry was nearly perfect. Mission Control predicted a smooth return home.

The confidence of Mission Control was short-lived. At 8:53 AM, various monitors at Mission Control began to flicker. The monitors showed that the temperature of the hydraulic systems in the ship's left wing had risen. This was not unusual. But only three minutes later, the temperature in the left landing gear and brake lining climbed an alarming 60 degrees (16°C).

Minutes later, *Columbia* was flying at an altitude of 40 miles (64 km), and traveling at 13,200 miles per hour (21,200 km/h). The space shuttle was just 1,400 miles (2,250 km) from home, or 16 minutes from landing. But the shuttle was experiencing trouble. The ship flew over Texas at an altitude of 207,000 feet (63,100 m). Mission Control communicator Charlie Hobaugh radioed the crew. "*Columbia*, Houston," he said, "we see your tire-pressure message."

Commander Husband started to reply when the communication lines suddenly fell silent. Above Texas, the shuttle disintegrated. There was a series of thundering booms. Showers of flaming debris fell from the sky over a 700-mile (1,130-km) section of Texas and Louisiana.

Mission Control was still unaware of the disaster. Hobaugh had tried to make contact with the ship. But there was only static. The rest of the ship's monitors also were dead. A mission that everyone thought would be flawless had taken a horrible turn. Mission Control realized that *Columbia* was gone. At last the announcer at Mission Control said a space-shuttle emergency had been declared.

At the Kennedy Space Center in Florida, spectators and members of the astronauts' families watched the sky for *Columbia*'s arrival. The families began to count down from ten to zero. When they reached zero, the sky was still empty. They listened carefully for the sound of sonic booms to signal the shuttle's return. But they heard nothing. They began to understand there was no one to wait for.

Opposite page: *Preflight systems checks showed no malfunctions with* Columbia.

SPACE PROGRAM BEGINNINGS

Today, space travel stands out as one the most impressive accomplishments of humankind. And the United States has become a world leader in space exploration. The United States, however, did not start out as the leader. In 1957, the Soviet Union—the United States's great rival—became the first country to put a man-made object in space.

On October 4, the Soviet Union launched a basketball-sized satellite called *Sputnik 1* into orbit. This was a year before the United States founded its own space program, the National Aeronautics and Space Administration (NASA).

NASA launched the first American satellite in 1958. Then the Soviets did one better. On April 12, 1961, Soviet cosmonaut Yury Gagarin became the first human in space. Gagarin circled Earth once before returning home. "Now let other countries try to catch us," Gagarin boasted.

Shortly after Gagarin's space flight, the United States launched the Mercury mission. It would launch America's first manned spacecraft. Alan Shepard became the first American in space on May 5, 1961.

Shepard's ride aboard *Freedom 7* lasted only 15 minutes. But the launch proved that the United States was still competitive in the space race. Project Mercury launched six manned ships over the next three years.

Cosmonaut Yury Gagarin

The United States responded to Gagarin's mission in another dramatic way. President John F. Kennedy wanted a mission that would propel the United States ahead of the Soviet Union in the space race.

Vice President Lyndon B. Johnson asked leaders in NASA and the military their opinions about what the United States should do to take the lead. Based on these opinions, Johnson told Kennedy the United States should try to put a man on the moon.

President Kennedy addresses the nation about the space program.

On May 25, 1961, Kennedy proposed a bold goal to Congress. He declared that the United States would attempt to land a man on the moon before the end of the decade. Kennedy said, "No single space project . . . will be more exciting, or more impressive to mankind, or more important . . . and none will be so difficult or expensive to accomplish."

NASA designed its next program, called Gemini, to prepare astronauts for landing on the moon. Astronauts learned how to fly a spacecraft in two ways. They practiced maneuvering spaceships while orbiting Earth. They also flew craft that docked with other space vehicles.

Ten Gemini missions took place over 20 months from 1965 to 1966. During one of these missions—*Gemini 8*—astronauts Neil Armstrong and David Scott almost lost consciousness when the ship spun out of control.

The Apollo project was the next stage of the lunar mission. The *Apollo 1* was a highly technical and complicated spacecraft. It contained almost 2 million working parts. Engineers began running tests on the ship, anticipating a launch in February 1967.

On January 27, engineers prepared to run a test to prove the spacecraft could function on its own power. Astronauts Virgil "Gus" Grissom, Edward White, and Roger Chaffee participated in the test.

Inside the ship, Grissom, White, and Chaffee monitored the spaceship's systems and went through checklists as if they were actually taking off. The test began in the morning and stretched into the evening.

Around 6:30 PM, the testing took a terrible turn. "We've got a fire in the spacecraft!" Chaffee cried over the radio circuit. During the test, the cabin's atmosphere had been replaced with pure oxygen. Given this condition, the cabin was highly flammable. Test crew workers desperately tried to open the *Apollo 1*'s hatches. But the doors were too hot to touch, and the smoke was too thick.

The workers continued to try to get the doors open. Five minutes passed before workers finally opened the hatches. Unfortunately, it was too late. Grissom, White, and Chaffee were dead. It was determined that they had died from inhaling toxic gases within the first 18 seconds of the fire.

The *Apollo 1* tragedy shocked the entire world. NASA conducted an investigation but never found out what caused the fire. However, the tragedy did bring important improvements to the Apollo Program. One of these changes was a better escape method.

After the tragedy, the space program had numerous successes. One of the most famous is the moon mission of *Apollo 11*. *Apollo 11* made a trip that placed the United States strides ahead in the space race.

On July 20, 1969, astronaut Neil Armstrong stepped off his lunar module vehicle and became the first man to set foot on the moon. Later, Edwin "Buzz" Aldrin joined him. The two men spent 21 hours on the moon's surface and collected almost 49 pounds (22 kg) of lunar rocks.

In November, *Apollo 12* followed in *Apollo 11*'s footsteps, giving NASA another successful moon landing. Then, another disaster struck on *Apollo 13*.

Buzz Aldrin walks on the moon near an American flag.

The crew of Apollo 11

NEIL ARMSTRONG

Neil Armstrong, the first man to walk on the moon, began his aviation career at an early age. He received his student's pilot's license before he passed his driving test. Armstrong went on to fly for the U.S. Navy from 1949 to 1952. During the Korean War, he flew 78 combat missions. In 1962, Armstrong was accepted into NASA's astronaut program. Armstrong lives in Ohio with his wife, Janet.

MICHAEL COLLINS

Michael Collins, who piloted the command module during the Apollo 11 mission, has an honored flying career. He was a fighter pilot and an experimental test pilot before becoming an astronaut in 1963. In July 1966, Collins and astronaut John Young commanded the Gemini 10 mission. Collins also served as director of the Smithsonian Institution's National Air and Space Museum from 1971 to 1978.

EDWIN ALDRIN

Edwin Aldrin, the second man to walk on the moon, has a scientific and military background. During the Korean War, he flew 66 combat missions. In 1963, Aldrin earned a degree in astronautics from the Massachusetts Institute of Technology. That same year, NASA selected Aldrin to become an astronaut. He flew on the final Gemini mission in 1966. Aldrin continues to lecture about space exploration.

"THAT'S ONE SMALL STEP FOR MAN, ONE GIANT LEAP FOR MANKIND."

Famous quote from Neil Armstrong upon walking on the moon

The *Apollo 13* mission was supposed to be the third flight to carry men to the moon's surface. Commander James Lovell Jr., Command Module Pilot John Swigert, and Lunar Module Pilot Fred Haise Jr. made up the *Apollo 13* crew.

On April 11, 1970, *Apollo 13* took off from Cape Canaveral, Florida. The first two days of the mission were problem free. Then, on the night of April 13, things began to go wrong.

Swigert made a routine stir of the oxygen tanks. During the procedure, a spark of electricity caused an explosion in one of the tanks. Swigert immediately radioed Mission Control. "Houston," he said, "we have a problem here."

At first, Mission Control thought *Apollo 13* had a simple instrument failure. But soon, two of the three fuel cells lost all power. The third cell also showed signs of weakening. A leak had been blown in the oxygen supply.

Oxygen was necessary for the fuel cells to function. This supply also provided the astronauts with their storage of oxygen to breathe. The astronauts' lives were in danger. They had to return to Earth immediately. No one knew if they could make it alive.

After three sleepless days, Lovell, Swigert, and Haise managed to navigate the ship back toward Earth. The crew reentered Earth's atmosphere around noon on Friday, April 17. During reentry, the spacecraft lost communication with Mission Control. More than a

The launch of Apollo 13

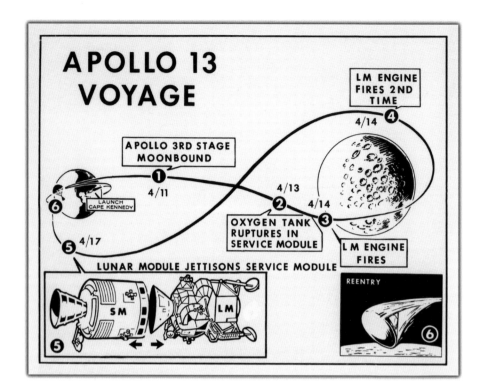

APOLLO 13 VOYAGE

APOLLO 3RD STAGE MOONBOUND ①
4/11

LAUNCH CAPE KENNEDY ⑥

4/13 ②

OXYGEN TANK RUPTURES IN SERVICE MODULE

4/14 ③

LM ENGINE FIRES 2ND TIME ④
4/14

LM ENGINE FIRES

4/17 ⑤

LUNAR MODULE JETTISONS SERVICE MODULE

SM   LM ⑤

REENTRY ⑥

Apollo 13's crew needed to use new techniques to return to Earth safely. This NASA diagram shows how the astronauts used the moon's gravity to catapult themselves back toward Earth. It also shows the lunar module detaching from the service module prior to reentry.

minute passed without word from the astronauts. Mission Control feared the worst.

The battered *Apollo 13* landed in the Pacific Ocean. At 12:07 PM, Swigert's voice came through to let Mission Control know the astronauts were still alive. Several minutes later, a U.S. ship rescued the three men. The United States had escaped a tragedy.

After the moon landings, the American public began to lose interest in the space program. Many felt that the United States was not getting much in return for the billions of dollars it was spending on space missions. NASA turned its attention from lunar landings to a space station called Skylab.

On May 14, 1973, NASA launched Skylab. It was important because it showed that humans could live in space for long periods of time. The first crew spent 28 days aboard the space station. The last crew lived in Skylab for 84 days.

NASA intended for Skylab to stay in orbit for several years. However, after high solar activity, Skylab returned to Earth's atmosphere and fell apart in July 1979. Debris from Skylab fell over remote areas of Australia and the Indian Ocean.

Skylab's existence ended prematurely, but the craft had proved its value. It is considered a forerunner to the International Space Station.

The Skylab space station in orbit above Earth

A NEW SPACESHIP

In the 1960s, engineers had begun wondering if it were possible to create a reusable spaceship. Spacecrafts of the day, such as *Saturn*, dumped most of their equipment into the ocean during the launch. Such ships were impractical and expensive to be used for frequent space travel.

NASA began developing a new kind of ship in the early 1970s that would be fully reusable. Engineers wanted to build a spacecraft in which both the booster and the orbiter could return to the launch site.

In 1971, NASA had developed a plan. The concept included a partially reusable system. One large fuel tank would drop after it emptied. Two other solid fuel boosters could be retrieved for future use. Engineers designed an orbiter that returned to a runway at the end of the mission. NASA referred to the vehicle as a Space Transportation System, or STS. This plan was the beginning of the space shuttle *Columbia*.

NASA contracted the North American Rockwell Corporation to build the orbiter. When it was finished, the orbiter was a monstrous 122 feet (37 m) long, with a wingspan of 78 feet (24 m). The cargo bay was 60 feet (18 m) long and 15 feet (4.6 m) wide. It was large enough to carry several satellites into orbit.

A replica of a space shuttle is displayed outside the U.S. Space and Rocket Center in Huntsville, Alabama. Named Pathfinder, *the replica shows guests the actual size of a space shuttle.*

The external fuel tank was 154 feet (47 m) long and held two internal tanks. One internal tank contained liquid hydrogen, and the other contained oxygen rocket fuel. With both tanks full, the entire ship weighed 1.7 million pounds (771,100 kg).

Building the shuttle was no small task. The spacecraft had 2.5 million parts, including 230 miles (370 km) of wire, 1,060 plumbing valves and connections, and 1,440 circuit breakers.

The Space Shuttle Main Engine (SSME) was 14 feet (4.3 m) tall and 8 feet (2.4 m) wide. It weighed 7,000 pounds (3,175 kg). More than half of *Columbia*'s power came from its three SSMEs. A high-pressure turbo pump drove each main engine. This thrust amounted to 77,000 horsepower for each pump.

Columbia sits on the launchpad at Kennedy Space Center in Cape Canaveral, Florida, before its first mission. It is the first space shuttle to be launched into space.

The shuttle's mission was to show that it could perform in space and return safely to Earth. During *Columbia*'s first mission, astronauts Robert Crippen and John Young orbited Earth for 54 hours before returning.

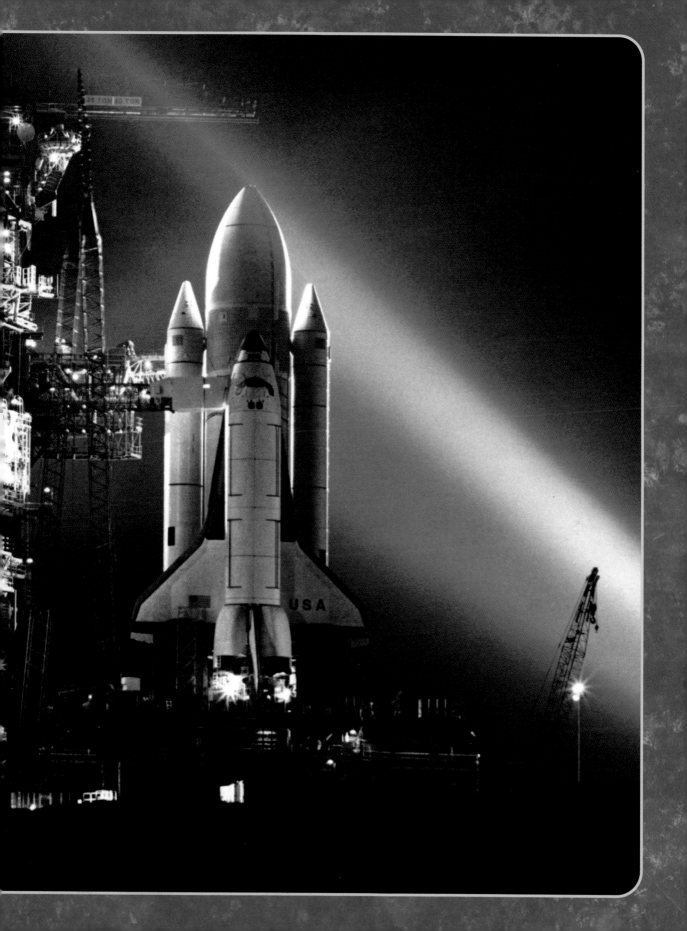

After multiple delays, *Columbia* was finally ready for the launchpad on April 12, 1981. The first of its kind, the space shuttle *Columbia* was sure to make history. Commanding the first flight was 50-year-old John Young, an Apollo and Gemini veteran. Robert Crippen, a 43-year-old navy captain and jet pilot, took the pilot's seat.

Columbia had a successful first mission. Both Young and Crippen were impressed. "The vehicle is performing like a champ," Young reported. On April 14, just two days after launch, *Columbia* touched down at Edwards Air Force Base in California.

The perfect landing was met with loud cheers from the crowd gathered around the base. Mission Control radioed the crew, "Welcome home, *Columbia*. Beautiful!"

Another shuttle that NASA developed was called *Challenger*. *Challenger* was first launched into space in 1983. By 1986, it had completed nine successful missions.

After a successful first mission, Columbia *approaches the landing strip at Edwards Air Force Base in southern California. It is escorted by a chase plane.*

On the morning of January 28, 1986, *Challenger* sat on the launchpad in preparation for its tenth mission. The morning was unusually cold in central Florida. Problems had delayed the launch for several months, and NASA was under pressure to get the shuttle off the ground.

This shuttle flight was of particular importance. It was the first mission to bring a civilian into space. Schoolteacher Christa McAuliffe had won a nationwide "Teacher in Space" contest. For months, she trained with the crew for her first space journey.

When the countdown reached zero, *Challenger*'s rockets roared. The ship lifted skyward. At first, the launch had appeared to go smoothly. At 70 seconds, the shuttle neared 50,000 feet (15,240 m).

Suddenly, the ship shook violently. Then it exploded in three plumes of smoke. The blazing plumes arched downward. On the ground, stunned spectators stood looking up at the sky.

Investigators later discovered that the cold weather had contributed to the explosion. The rubber O-rings in the rocket boosters had not been able to expand properly because of the cold. Flames from the booster shot out of the gaps, causing a tremendous burst of fire.

After the *Challenger* disaster, no space shuttles flew for 32 months. During part of that time, NASA conducted an investigation of the *Challenger* disaster. But the space program continued. In September 1988, the space shuttle *Discovery* made the first shuttle flight since the disaster.

Columbia did not resume flight until August 1989. However, the space shuttle continued to make history. Eileen Collins was the first woman to command a space shuttle during a *Columbia* mission in 1999. In early 2003, *Columbia* took off on its twenty-eighth and final flight.

THE SEVEN ASTRONAUTS

The seven men and women who boarded *Columbia* did not see themselves as heroes, but as ordinary people doing a job they loved. Here are the stories of these astronauts.

Ever since he was a little boy, Mission Commander Rick Husband wanted to be an astronaut. In 1999, Husband rode *Discovery* into space. He got a chance to fly *Discovery*. He took the ship around the space station two and a half times. As he steered the spacecraft, he turned around and exclaimed, "This is so much fun!"

After that mission, NASA chose Husband to command *Columbia* on STS-107. Space shuttle missions are labeled STS followed by a mission number.

Columbia Pilot William C. "Willie" McCool was also passionate about reaching the sky. As a child, McCool fell in love with building model airplanes. This hobby was an early clue that McCool would make flying his life's work.

McCool kept his sense of humor when describing what it was like in space. "I'll tell you," he said, "there's nothing better than listening to a good album and looking out the windows and watching the world go by while you pedal on the [exercise] bike."

Columbia's crew members prepare to board the shuttle. From front left: Mission Specialists Kalpana Chawla, Pilot William C. McCool, Commander Rick Husband. Back left: Payload Specialist Ilan Ramon, Payload Commander Michael Anderson, Mission Specialist David Brown. Center: Mission Specialist Laurel Blair Salton Clark.

*Chawla before her first
mission on STS-87*

Kalpana Chawla decided to become an aerospace engineer when she was in the tenth grade. Chawla grew up in Karnal, India, a small town near New Delhi.

Because India did not have an aerospace program, Chawla decided to emigrate to the United States. She entered the astronaut program in 1994.

Chawla's first space mission was in 1997 aboard *Columbia* on STS-87. Like her 2003 trip, this flight was a 16-day science mission. Her flight made her the first Indian-born woman to fly into space. In India, her hometown honored this accomplishment with a torchlight parade. She was a national hero.

Columbia also served as a historic moment for another astronaut. Ilan Ramon became the first Israeli astronaut to go into space during the 2003 mission. He grew up in a suburb of Tel Aviv, Israel, and served in the Israeli Air Force.

In 1997, Ramon received a phone call inviting him to apply to become an astronaut. Ramon thought the call was a joke because in Hebrew the word *astronaut* can also mean someone who is lost in his or her thoughts. When he was accepted as Israel's first astronaut, he jumped up in excitement.

It was a great honor for Ramon to represent his country aboard *Columbia*. During the flight, Ramon sent an inspiring e-mail to his nation. In the message, Ramon wrote that Israel was beautiful

The space shuttle Columbia's crew poses for a photo during its mission in January 2003.

┌ DID YOU KNOW? ┐

Did you know that floating in space can affect the health of astronauts? Although weightlessness looks like a lot of fun, it actually has some unpleasant and dangerous side effects. Astronauts lose muscle tone and bone mass in space because floating doesn't allow them to do weight-bearing exercise. They can also become slightly anemic, and many experience nausea. Most of these problems are easily dealt with when astronauts return to Earth. But no one is sure if living in space longer than a year would cause permanent damage to astronauts' bodies.

William McCool   Rick Husband   Ilan Ramon   Kalpana Chawla

from space. The quietness of space added to his country's beauty. He hoped that someday this peacefulness might reach Israel.

Mission Specialist David Brown also took an unusual path to the space program. For this reason, he was sometimes called "the accidental astronaut."

During high school, Brown became a star gymnast. He joined the circus while he attended college. Brown juggled, walked on stilts, and rode a unicycle. He later attended medical school and became a navy flight surgeon. NASA selected Brown for the astronaut program in 1996. Crazy about space, he kept a telescope in his living room pointed at the moon.

On his first and only shuttle mission, Brown carried a small flag from his high school in Arlington, Virginia. Fellow graduates had carried a flag to the summit of Mount Everest. Before the flight, Brown had joked, "I'm going to get it a little bit higher up, but I won't have to walk as far to get it there."

Laurel Blair Salton Clark was also one who aimed high. She grew up in Racine, Wisconsin. Clark constantly looked for new ways to challenge herself. Little did she know her drive would lead her to

David Brown   Laurel Clark   Michael Anderson   Mission Insignia

the space program. She recalled getting excited about the moon landings, but she did not consider becoming an astronaut.

After she learned exactly what astronauts do, she became more interested in space. Clark began training as an astronaut in 1996. She served on *Columbia* as a mission specialist.

Unlike Clark, Payload Commander Michael Anderson dreamed of being in space at an early age. As a child, he enjoyed watching the television programs *Star Trek* and *Lost in Space.*

In 1998, Anderson had his first space flight aboard the space shuttle *Endeavour.* During the STS-89 mission, *Endeavour* made a 10-day stop at the Russian space station *Mir.*

Anderson's stay made him the first African American to visit a space station. He took pride in being a role model for young people, because he felt it was important to inspire children to learn.

On *Columbia*, Anderson oversaw the science experiments. Even though he believed in the importance of space missions, he knew that it was a dangerous job. "I'll take the risk," he said, "because I think what we're doing is really important."

SIXTEEN DAYS IN SPACE

The *Columbia* astronauts kept busy during their 16-day journey in space. They performed many scientific experiments and took pictures of Earth. As exciting as the trip in space must have been, *Columbia's* crew knew it had important work to do.

The crew conducted more than 80 different studies. Some experiments would be conducted in Spacehab. Spacehab is a pressurized science lab. Other space shuttles had used Spacehab. However, this was the first time Spacehab was aboard *Columbia*.

Ramon performed an experiment on soot. In zero gravity, flames are symmetrical and even. For this reason, Ramon could look more closely at how a flame produces soot.

On Earth, soot is a major pollutant. Ramon hoped to gather data that would be useful to U.S. aircraft engine manufacturers. The experiment could help create aircraft engines that produce little soot.

Some crew members performed biology experiments. They were interested in how the body functions in space. Crew members took turns drawing each other's blood. Then they examined how the body uses protein and calcium in a zero-gravity environment. They also studied how bone loss occurs in space.

One of *Columbia's* medical experiments focused on cancer. Clark monitored cancer cells using the Bioreactor Demonstration System.

Columbia *crew members give a thumbs up after
successfully completing an experiment in the Spacehab.*

This device can grow biological cultures much better than laboratories on Earth. Clark reported a cancer tumor as large as a golf ball. This sample was the largest ever grown in space.

Columbia also carried six experiments from around the world. They had experiments from Australia, China, Israel, Japan, and the United States. The studies were part of the Space Technology and Research Students program, or STARS. Crew members studied how space affected the lives of fish, bees, ants, and silkworms. They also watched a spider build a web in zero gravity.

As the 16 days drew to a close, the *Columbia*'s crew felt the mission had been a success. The crew members were impressed by the number of experiments conducted in such a short time. They believed that many great discoveries could be made in future space missions. Anderson said, "I think once we get a seven-member crew on board the space station you're really going to see some outstanding science in space."

During the last day in space the crew began planning for reentry and landing. Husband and Chawla took turns practicing landing with an onboard computer training system called PILOT. The astronauts concluded any remaining experiments. Then they performed some preliminary checks for reentry. Weather forecasts predicted ideal conditions for touchdown at the Kennedy Space Center. Winds would be light with few clouds in the sky.

On Saturday, February 1, 2003, *Columbia*'s reentry seemed normal until a monitor indicated trouble. Some of the data collected during the 16-day mission blew apart with the ship. However, the discoveries of the *Columbia* mission were not all lost. Many reports had already been downloaded to Mission Control. For the seven astronauts, the flight was not in vain.

KENNEDY SPACE CENTER

A shuttle outside the Vehicle Assembly Building at the Kennedy Space Center

An aerial view of the Kennedy Space Center visitor's area

The Kennedy Space Center is NASA's main launching site. It is located near Orlando, Florida, on Merritt Island. In the early 1960s, NASA needed to find a large launching site as it developed the Apollo moon mission. Dr. Kurt H. Debus of NASA and Lieutenant General Leighton I. Davis of the U.S. Department of Defense joined forces to select a suitable site.

Debus and Davis considered many places, including Hawaii, a few Caribbean islands, and the California coast. They decided Merritt Island was the best choice because it is close to Cape Canaveral. The site was initially called the Launch Operations Center. In December 1963, it was renamed the Kennedy Space Center to honor the slain president, John F. Kennedy.

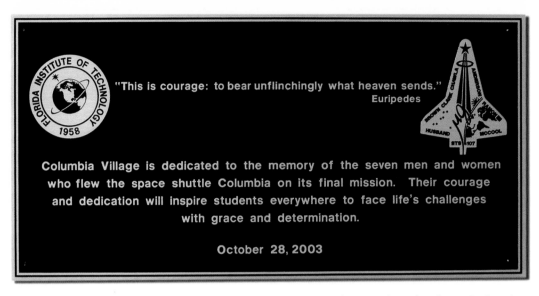

A plaque commemorating the seven crew members who died on Columbia

Family members did their best to be strong, and they tried to understand the greater purpose their loved ones served. Two days after the *Columbia* disaster, Evelyn Husband, wife of Commander Rick Husband, read a statement from the families: "On January 16 we saw our loved ones launch into a brilliant, cloud-free sky. Their hearts were full of enthusiasm, pride in country, faith in their God and a willingness to accept risk in the pursuit of knowledge— knowledge that might improve the quality of life for all mankind."

The United States mourned the loss of *Columbia*'s crew members. On February 4, a memorial service took place at NASA's Johnson Space Center in Houston, Texas. More than 7,000 aerospace workers attended, as well as the families of the *Columbia* astronauts.

President George W. Bush gave his condolences to the mourners. "Today we remember not only one moment of tragedy, but seven lives of great purpose and achievement." After he finished speaking, a bell rang seven times in memory of the seven astronauts. Mourners then looked up to the sky as four T-38 jets roared above them in the "missing man" formation.

President George W. Bush speaks at the memorial service in Houston, Texas, at NASA's Johnson Space Center.

THE SEARCH FOR ANSWERS

After the *Columbia* disaster, people began searching for clues about why it happened. They started studying what remained of the space shuttle.

Minutes after *Columbia*'s disintegration, hundreds of pieces of flaming debris had fallen on Texas and Louisiana. The area of land hit by smoking chunks of torn metal totaled more than 500 square miles (1,295 sq km). Pieces of the shuttle struck homes, businesses, and schools. Luckily, no one on the ground was injured.

Search teams of law enforcement officers, firefighters, and National Guard members combed the countryside. In less than a week, searchers collected more than 12,000 pieces of shuttle debris. Among the pieces was a 700-pound (318-kg) rocket engine.

Unfortunately, some people who found pieces of the shuttle wanted to keep them as mementos. NASA officials pleaded with anyone who was holding debris to bring it in. They reasoned that these fragments might offer clues that could prevent future disasters.

All debris was transported to the Kennedy Space Center in Florida. There, investigators laid out each piece by its location on the shuttle. Little by little, they tried to put the ship back together. Investigators hoped to find clues as to why the shuttle exploded.

Debris from Columbia *is laid out on a grid at the Reusable Launch Vehicle Hangar at Kennedy Space Center to determine the cause of the accident.*

One theory was that space debris or a tiny meteor struck *Columbia*. That theory did not gain much support. Before liftoff, the U.S. Air Force and NASA examined the shuttle's orbit for any objects that might collide with the spacecraft.

Most evidence points to a problem with *Columbia*'s left wing. Special tiles on the shuttle help insulate the spacecraft from reentry heat caused by atmospheric friction. If any of the tiles are damaged during launch or while in space, important equipment could be damaged by the extreme heat.

Scientists believe that a hole in the left wing may have caused heat to penetrate the shuttle's skin. The temperature would be great enough to melt wires and girders in the shuttle's wing.

Firefighters walk shoulder-to-shoulder searching for debris from the *Columbia* disaster. More than 16,500 people searched 680,700 acres (275,470 ha) of land to find pieces of the shuttle. Even with all these people, it took three months to complete the search. The search groups found more than 82,500 pieces of debris. Altogether, the debris weighed 84,800 pounds (38,460 kg). This is about 40 percent of the original weight of *Columbia*.

Soon after the accident, NASA announced the creation of a panel to investigate the disaster. The committee was called the Columbia Accident Investigation Board. Harold W. Gehman, a retired admiral, was in the charge of the board made up of military officials and safety experts.

In June, NASA released videotapes and photographs taken by *Columbia*'s astronauts. These pictures were released after the Columbia Accident Investigation Board decided the images would not help its inquiry. The footage included about 10 hours of video and 92 photographs that were found among the debris.

In total, *Columbia*'s astronauts had taken 337 videotapes and 137 rolls of film, but only some of the images were recovered. Most of the images show the astronauts conducting experiments and going about everyday life on the space shuttle.

The Columbia Accident Investigation Board's inquiry lasted almost seven months and cost $400 million. About 400 NASA engineers worked with the board on the investigation. On August 26, 2003, the board issued its final report.

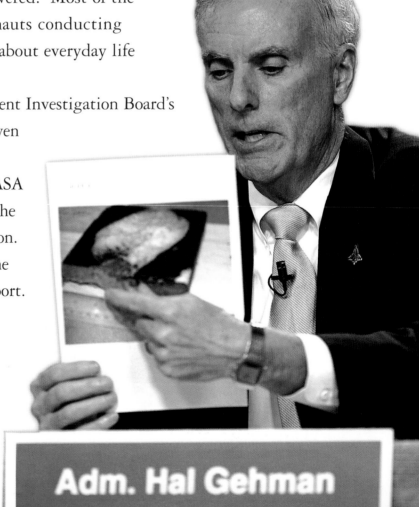

The chairman of the Columbia Accident Investigation Board, Harold W. Gehman, presents evidence during a press conference at Johnson Space Center.

Adm. Hal Gehman

Despite preflight diagnostic tests, the Columbia *shuttle and its crew could not be saved from disaster.*

The 248-page report confirmed NASA's theory about the cause of the accident. According to the report, about 82 seconds into the flight a chunk of foam had fallen from the fuel tank. The foam hit the left wing, gouging a hole into the wing's surface.

The board, however, had done more than examine the physical cause of the accident. In its report, the board also criticized NASA for beginning to minimize the dangers of space travel. Some NASA engineers had suspected something had gone wrong during liftoff, the report noted. But NASA managers had stifled those concerns.

The report also made a series of recommendations for preventing future space shuttle disasters. NASA was encouraged to implement some recommendations before the next space shuttle flight. Many short-term proposals called for improving the shuttle's structure and for collecting better images of the shuttle during liftoff.

Despite the tragedy, space exploration continues to inspire the world. Outstanding men and women step up to take the places of the heroes who journeyed into space before them. As President Bush assured mourners in Houston, "Although we grieve deeply . . . the bold exploration of space must go on."

TIMELINE

1957 The Soviet Union launches the first Earth orbiter, *Sputnik 1.*

1958 The National Aeronautics and Space Administration (NASA) is founded. The first U.S. satellite goes into orbit.

1961 On April 12, Soviet cosmonaut Yury Gagarin becomes the first man in space aboard *Vostok 1.* Alan Shepard becomes the first American in space on May 5 during Project Mercury.

1965 United States begins the Gemini missions.

1967 The *Apollo 1* fire causes the death of three astronauts.

1969 On July 20, astronauts Neil Armstrong and Edwin "Buzz" Aldrin become the first men to set foot on the moon.

1970   *Apollo 13* escapes a tragedy.

1981   In April, the space shuttle *Columbia* successfully completes its first mission, becoming the world's first reusable spacecraft.

1983   The space shuttle *Challenger* takes its first flight.

1986   On January 28, *Challenger* explodes 73 seconds after liftoff, claiming the lives of seven astronauts.

2003   On February 1, *Columbia* disintegrates during reentry only 16 minutes from landing.

        On August 26, the Columbia Accident Investigation Board issues its report.

American Moments

FAST FACTS

In 1792, a ship called *Columbia* sailed up a river in the Pacific Northwest. The river was named the Columbia River after the ship. Later, the space shuttle *Columbia* was named after the ship, too.

The six original space shuttle orbiters were *Atlantis*, *Challenger*, *Columbia*, *Discovery*, *Endeavour*, and *Enterprise*. *Enterprise* was a test vehicle not designed for space flight.

In 1996, the *Columbia* set a record for the longest space shuttle flight with a 17-day mission. The flight lasted from November 19 to December 7. The shuttle had been scheduled to land earlier, but poor weather had delayed the landing.

After the *Columbia* tragedy, some people hoped to profit from the disaster by selling debris. An eBay listing appeared for an item that was claimed to be from *Columbia*. The opening bid was $10,000. Officials from eBay quickly removed the listing. The U.S. government vowed to prosecute anyone selling the *Columbia*'s debris.

In 36 years of space exploration, 23 astronauts in the American space program have lost their lives during in-flight and training accidents.

Would you like to learn more about the Space Shuttle Columbia Disaster? Please visit **www.abdopub.com** to find up-to-date Web site links about the Space Shuttle Columbia Disaster and other American moments. These links are routinely monitored and updated to provide the most current information available.

Columbia lifted off on November 11, 1982. It carried the first commercial satellites in the history of the STS program and the first four-person crew in a single launch in the history of space flight.

GLOSSARY

aerospace engineer: an engineer who makes airplanes or space ships.

anemia: a condition where the blood has a low red blood cell count. It can also mean the hemoglobin level, or the whole blood volume, is low.

booster: a rocket that helps provide thrust during a space shuttle's liftoff. After liftoff, the two boosters drop off and land by parachute.

cosmonaut: an astronaut from the Soviet Union.

debris: pieces of rock or another substance or object that have been broken apart.

girder: a support beam.

lunar: having to do with the moon.

module: part of a space vehicle that can detach and be piloted separately.

orbit: to revolve around.

orbiter: a spacecraft that is built to orbit planets, moons, or stars but not to land on them. An orbiter can carry parts of a laboratory or space station. It can also carry satellites.

plasma stage: a period in which plasma, or heated gases, surround the space shuttle during its return to Earth.

reentry: to return to Earth's atmosphere from space.

sonic boom: a sound like an explosion made by something going faster than the speed of sound. The shock wave coming off the nose of a space shuttle upon reentry makes a sonic boom when the wave hits the ground.

zero gravity: a condition in which the force of orbital flight causes an apparent lack of gravity.

The Columbia *crew eats breakfast together the morning of the launch.*

INDEX